THE ANXIETY RELIEF SCRIPTURES

The 30-Day Daily Devotional for Overcoming Anxiety and Worry

Kimberly Taylor

TakeBackYourTemple.com

Please see your health care provider for diagnosis and treatment of any medical concerns, and before implementing any nutrition, exercise or other lifestyle changes.

Table of Contents

Day 1: Stay Prayed Up

Today's focus scripture is taken from Philippians 4:6-7 ~ ⚠

> "Be anxious for nothing, but in everything by prayer and supplication, with thanksgiving, let your requests be made known to God; and the peace of God, which surpasses all understanding, will guard your hearts and minds through Christ Jesus."

According to author Bob Beaudine, anxiety occurs when you believe your nightmares instead of your dreams. It affects your physical and mental well-being.

However there is one area that it doesn't affect – your Spiritual well-being. Or at least it doesn't affect it **directly**, although it can indirectly. I'll explain more about that later.

The reason why anxiety cannot affect your Spiritual well-being directly is because the Holy Spirit makes this part of you alive – which is the same Spirit that raised Jesus from the dead!

Because the Holy Spirit is aware of things to come, He can't be anxious about the future. He is in perfect peace. He is of one mind with the Father and the Son and knows the ultimate plan for your life. He knows anything happening to you now is just temporary, a part of your life story.

Have you sought the Lord in prayer about His purpose for your life? Are you confident that the place you are and the people you are with are those in line with that purpose? Many people suffer from needless stress, worry, and anxiety because they are in places and with people God never intended for them!

I listened to pastor Robert Morris teach about how we need to raise the level of prayer in our lives. He said something that made me smile: "Prayer is transferring your burdens to the Lord. If you've prayed and you are still carrying the burden afterwards, you didn't really pray; you just griped."

He joked about a man who spoke to him about a problem he was having and he asked the man, "Have you transferred it to the Lord?" The man answered, "Yes, I have. Many times!" I laughed because many times I called myself giving a problem to the Lord – only to take it back.

This relates to the potential problem I mentioned earlier about anxiety affecting your Spiritual well-being indirectly. If you are not practicing Spiritual disciplines like prayer, praise, worship, and study of God's word daily, then your Spirit man will weaken. You won't be able to handle life's challenges in a way that glorifies God.

These disciplines are Spiritual food for you, and just like physical food feeds your physical being, Spiritual food feeds your Spiritual being.

So the more anxious you are, the more you need to redirect that energy into prayer and praise. Double the anxiety? Double the prayer! Use your prayer time to ask God to show you His purpose for your life and His viewpoint on the situations you are dealing with. Even if you are feeling shaky, let the word of the Lord settle the matter.

The Lord will sustain you, no matter what the circumstances look like. Let the Spirit guide you; sometimes He'll direct you as to an action to take and sometimes, He'll direct you to stand still and see the Salvation of the Lord.

Always pray with a thankful heart; everything that you have is a result of God's supply. He is the ultimate source, not money, a job, career, relationship, a perfect clothing size, or anything else. Once that fact becomes a reality to you, then God's peace will sustain you.

1) Tell God what I'm worried about.
2) Tell God what I would like to happen
3) Give Thanks
4) Think of Something potives.

John 14:27

Peace I leave with you; my peace
I give to you. I do not give to you
as the world gives. Do not let your
hearts be troubled, and do not let
them be afraid.

8

Day 2: God Anchors You

Today's focus scripture is taken from Psalm 55:22

> *worries*
> "Cast your burden on the Lord, And He
> *Strengthen*
> shall sustain you; He shall never permit
> the righteous to be moved"
> *one / person*

A lady recently wrote to me about the turmoil going on in her life. She described her emotional state as "like waves tossed to and fro."

Sounds like a lot of moving, doesn't it? Anxiety can cause emotional instability and when you are unstable, you are most likely to make decisions that you will regret later.

Thinking about her description, I also remembered the scripture from James 1:5-6. In the first part of the scripture, he advises us to ask God for wisdom. But then, he gives a warning:

> "But let him ask in faith, with no doubting, for he who doubts is like a wave of the sea driven and tossed by the wind. For let not that man suppose that he will receive anything from the Lord; he is a double-minded man, unstable in all his ways."

So this lady's description of her emotional state as like "waves tossed to and fro" tells me that doubt is ruling her mind at the moment. Boy have I been there!

I used to be particularly vulnerable to this emotion around income tax season. Because I am self-employed, I reacted with fear, anxiety, and worry over any potential tax bill.

But a few years ago, when I felt my old emotional reactions rise up, something even stronger rose up inside me at the same time. It was like a big stop sign that brought those feelings to a halt by commanding "Stop. You are not going there."

This new determination to control my emotions surprised me. And you know what? It felt great!

In that moment, I was determined to set my mind on faith. I would be single-minded. I was determined to trust the situation to God no matter how I felt.

God taught me something important during that experience: "Faith is a supernatural act."

I recently studied the story again of how God commanded the Israelites to go in to possess the Promised Land (see Numbers, chapter 13). Unfortunately, they chose to do the natural thing: they looked at the giants in the land and compared themselves to them. And because they saw themselves smaller in comparison, they reacted with fear and refused to do what God called them to do.

If you limit your mind to the natural, then you narrow the options that God has to change your situation. But if you elevate your mind to the supernatural realm through faith, then you are able to take action based on confidence in God's care for you.

So keep in mind: When you become single-minded, keeping your mind stayed on God's word and refuse to be moved, then you open the door for God to move in supernatural ways on your behalf!

Day 3: God Perfects your Concerns

Today's focus scripture is taken from Psalm 138:8

"The Lord will perfect that which concerns me; Your mercy, O Lord, endures forever; Do not forsake the works of Your hands."

[handwritten annotations: "For fill his purpose for me", "perfect", "last", "begin. Abandon me", "Gods"]

I once heard **worry** compared to a rocking chair. You can rock as much as you want to, but you'll never get anywhere!

It took me years to learn this lesson. Today's scripture is one that helped me greatly. Saying to myself, "The Lord will perfect that which concerns me" is my go-to affirmation now when anxiety or worry try to overtake my mind.

When I first decided to overcome the worrying habit, I used to questioned the scripture's truth. What if the Lord doesn't come through and the worst happens?

Then, I recalled the story of Shadrach, Meshach and Abed-Nego, the Hebrews who refused to bow down to worship the king's golden statue (see Daniel, chapter 3).

Many times, their story is used as an example of faith but consider their response when the king said that he would kill them if they did not worship his image:

> "… If that is the case, our God whom we serve is able to deliver us from the burning fiery furnace, and He will deliver us from your hand, O king. But if not, let it be known to you, O king, that we do not serve your gods, nor will we worship the gold image which you have set up."

They spoke in faith, but they also knew that God is sovereign and the ultimate decision on **how and when** to move is His. Yet, they

acted in faith anyway because it was the right
thing to do.

So starting now, I dare you to believe that God
will deliver you in your seemingly impossible
situation. I dare you to stand in faith so that
God has every option to act in your life – which
includes natural **and** supernatural ways.

Even when it is hard to stand in faith, continue
to do so. It is the right thing to do and it
pleases God:

> Hebrews 11:6; "But without faith it is
> impossible to please Him, for he who
> comes to God must believe that He is,
> and that He is a rewarder of those who
> diligently seek Him."

Starting now, won't you join me and dare to
put supernatural faith to the test and see God's
power move in your life? Get a piece of paper
and a pen and write down everything that you
are worried about or that makes you afraid.
Let God know what is on your heart. He

doesn't care about grammar or how you write. All He cares about is one of His children is seeking Him. Nobody needs to see what you wrote but you.

Writing everything down can help you see clearly about what is going on in your mind – and start to make sense of it. When you write it down, it has less power over you because you can see the words in black and white and be able to tell if what you wrote is the truth or a lie.

Also, write down what you hope your future will be - after seeking the Lord for direction. That will encourage you and help you to make wise choices. Are you willing to do that today? Don't delay. God will perfect everything that concerns you!

Day 4: Walk in the Spirit

Today's focus scripture is taken from Isaiah 40:31

"But those who wait on the Lord Shall renew their strength; They shall mount up with wings like eagles, They shall run and not be weary, They shall walk and not faint."

You may have heard today's scripture before, but have you ever wondered **how** to wait on the Lord to move in your situation? Surely you have better things to do than pacing the floor and wringing your hands!

Thankfully, the bible gives you wisdom about what to do to endure the wait:

1. **Seek the Lord before any decision.** In Ephesians 5:17, we are advised, "Therefore do not be unwise, but understand what the will of the Lord is."

The key word here is '**understand**'. Who knows the mind of the Lord better than the Spirit of the Lord? As a believer in Jesus Christ, you have the Holy Spirit living in you and dwelling with you. The Holy Spirit's role is to guide you and tell you things to come (see John 14:17 and John 16:13).

If you rely only on your human understanding when making decisions, it's like viewing the situation through a peephole. But when you ask the Lord in prayer for guidance before making a decision, the Holy Spirit will reveal to you the Godly answer, the panoramic view. Your job is to wait until you receive that answer. Peace and confidence in your Spirit accompanies the Godly answer.

It may be outside of your comfort zone, but your Spirit will know it is the right thing to do. Before you act, ask!

2. **Walk in the Spirit.** The bible promises that when you walk in the Spirit, you will not fulfill the lust of the flesh. Why is this important?

When you are anxious or worried, you are more likely to do things to relieve tension that might feel good now, but destructive later, such as overeating, excessive drinking or other fleshly behavior.

Ephesians 5:18-21 advises "And do not be drunk with wine, in which is dissipation; but be filled with the Spirit, speaking to one another in psalms and hymns and spiritual songs, singing and making melody in your heart to the Lord, giving thanks always for all things to God the Father in the name of our Lord Jesus Christ, submitting to one another in the fear of God." honor

So, here is what walking in the Spirit looks like in your daily life:

Encouraging others: Speak grace-filled words to others, encouraging them in their walk with the Lord. If you are around others who don't know the Lord, then plant seeds that will encourage them such as your testimony or biblical wisdom for the situation they are facing as the Holy Spirit leads you.

Keeping a praise song in your heart: You have the garment of praise for the Spirit of heaviness according to scripture. In your heart and mind, praise the Lord for who He is and what He has done for you. Doing it in song makes it even more meaningful and memorable.

Being thankful: Actively look for things to be thankful for throughout the day. When I was striving to overcome anxiety and depression, I made it a game to write down 7 things each day that I was thankful for. It is a powerful habit for me now to thank the Lord regularly throughout the day.

Being humble in your dealings with others: Be kind, courteous, and considerate to others, keeping in mind that you represent the Lord Jesus. The bible says that we should love our neighbor as ourselves. Let love lead you in your actions with others. People pay far more attention to what you do than what you say.

When you focus your mind and actions on doing these things rather than the wasteful activity of worry and destructive behavior, then you will have new strength and be ready to do whatever the Lord calls you to do!

Day 5: Accept Jesus' Peace

Today's focus scripture is taken from John 14:27

> "Peace I leave with you, My peace I give to you; not as the world gives do I give to you. Let not your heart be troubled, neither let it be afraid."

We all like to receive gifts, but have you received the gift that Jesus left you? In John 14:27, He assures you that he left you his peace. He also says to "let not" your heart be troubled nor afraid. The phrase "let not" means that this is something within your control.

When I read this scripture, I immediately thought about the story of Jesus walking on troubled waters (see Matthew 14:22-33). In the story, Peter also walked on the troubled waters for a brief time as he kept his focus on Jesus. But when he started regarding the circumstances (the wind and waves), he begin to sink.

Jesus is the author and finisher of your faith. So when you start regarding your circumstances above your God, you will feel like you are sinking too. But when focus on Him, your faith strengthens and His peace becomes your peace!

Consider the words of the popular hymn, "What a Friend We Have in Jesus":

"What a friend we have in Jesus,

All our sins and griefs to bear!

What a privilege to carry

Everything to God in prayer!

Oh, what peace we often forfeit,

Oh, what needless pain we bear,

All because we do not carry

Everything to God in prayer!"

This hymn contains the secret of receiving Jesus' peace: You recognize that Jesus carries your sins and sorrows. Your job is to carry your burdens to the Lord in prayer. Everything! There is no concern that you have that is too small or large for you to carry to the Lord.

Whenever you feel burdened or troubled, use that as your signal to fix your eyes on Jesus and pray as a means to transfer your burden to the Lord. Just like Jesus commanded, "Peace, be still" to the storm in Mark 4:39, so you invite Him into your situation to restore calm in your storm.

Day 6: The Lord is your Cover

Today's focus scripture is taken from Psalm 91:1-2

"He who dwells in the secret place of the Most High

Shall abide under the shadow of the Almighty.

I will say of the Lord, "He is my refuge and my fortress; My God, in Him I will trust."

In the U.S., we call *911* for emergency help. When we call 911, the dispatcher will send whatever emergency personnel is best for the situation – whether it be ambulance, police, or firefighters.

Just as you have confidence that 911 can help you in time of physical need, have that same confidence that Psalm 911 (for Psalm 91) can help you in time of Spiritual need!

I felt led to make this today's focus scripture after reading a question on Facebook. A young woman posted on her profile, "Who wants to be my cover?" Not being familiar with youth slang, I concluded that she was soliciting for a date or boyfriend. When I read it, my first thought was, "Jesus is the cover you need."

A cover is designed to conceal, to protect. In Psalm 91, many synonyms for cover are given. *Refuge* and *fortress* are just two of them. However to stay protected, your job is to dwell (live) in the secret place of the most high – that is, at the center of God's will for your life. You listen to the guidance of the Holy Spirit and you obey His leading. Under the shadow of the Almighty is the safest place you can be.

The Psalmist says that He will trust in God. But, it is hard to trust someone that you don't know. So take time to get to know God's character through the person of Jesus Christ. One of the best places to start is the book of John in the bible. You will see Jesus' loving heart in action and you will see His obedience to the Father modeled for you – even to the cross. You will see that He loved you so much that He gave His life for you.

And if He was willing to give His life for you, how much more will He care for you as you deal with the problems of this world?

When you recognize that the Lord is your cover, you can face life without worry and anxiety as to what might happen. You may not know the future, but you know the one who does. Past, present, and future – He's got you covered!

Day 7: Hope in the WORD

Today's focus scripture is taken from Psalm 130:5

> "I wait for the Lord, my soul waits, And in His word I do hope."

Gods coming and Gods word,

When meditating on this scripture, it occurred to me that your Spirit man has no problem waiting for breakthroughs. However, your soul (mind, will, and emotions) may become discouraged while waiting. Once, I dissected the word "dis-couraged" to mean "To take courage away." Whenever I start doubting that what I am believing for is going to happen, then I become discouraged, thinking "What's the use?"

Hope is the antidote to discouragement. The best source of hope is God's word. One of the scriptures that gives me great encouragement is Numbers 23:19: "God is not a man, that He should lie, Nor a son of man, that He should repent. Has He said, and will He not do? Or has He spoken, and will He not make it good?"

In this scripture, you see that hoping in God's word hinges on your belief that God **keeps** His word. The bible says that He is ready to perform it. So you have a choice to make: Do you believe in your temporary feelings more than God's permanent word?

I recommend finding scriptures that correspond to what you are hoping for in the bible. For example, let's say that you are believing for a financial breakthrough. A scripture you may hope in is, "And my God shall supply all your need according to His riches in glory by Christ Jesus (Philippians 4:19)." You can have confidence in this as long as you are in the place where God has placed you. If you are not sure, ask in prayer!

Use your imagination to paint a picture of God supplying your financial need as His word says He will. Whenever you find yourself becoming discouraged, re-affirm that scripture and see the mental picture you've created of it coming to pass.

I believe the highest use of the imagination is to use it to bolster Godly hope. Unfortunately, it's often misused by imagining the worst happening in your situation, causing worry, fear, and discouragement.

Why choose to live in that state? Instead, make the effort to channel your mental energy into hoping in God's word. You will experience more peace and it will make it easier to endure the wait.

Day 8: Believe in God's Care

Today's focus scripture is taken from 1 Peter 5:7

"Casting all your care upon him; for he cares for you."

It's natural to be concerned about your health, protection, and other things related to your welfare. However, this scripture tells you that you should put the ultimate responsibility for your care upon the Lord. Could it be that you are feeling burdened right now because you are trying to carry a load that you were never meant to carry?

25 - 33

In Matthew 6:26-30, Jesus gives two examples of how God cares for things in nature:

- He cares for the birds of the air, providing food for them

- He cares for the lilies of the field,
  clothing them with splendor

  extream Beauty (handwritten)

Jesus states that you, as God's child, are of much more value than birds or flowers so how **much more** will God care for you? While you still have a responsibility to use your God-given talents to benefit others and earn an income, it is ultimately God's responsibility to guide you to the opportunities that He has already prepared for you. Your responsibility is to listen for His guidance and follow His leading.

Consider this: You can deal with most of your concerns in life by asking yourself the following question: "Can I do something about this or not?"

- If you can do something about it — act according to God's guidance

- If you can't do something about it — give it to God in prayer, trusting that He'll work it out for your good

It's smart to save your energy for those things that you can actually do something about. You will experience more peace and contentment that way.

If you don't have the power to change the situation, then acknowledge that fact and turn it over to God in prayer. He has greater influence than you could ever hope to have. Don't waste your time with worrying. Take your burden and cast it on the Lord. I promise you – His shoulders are wide enough to carry it!

Day 9: Seek God's Kingdom Today

Today's focus scripture is taken from Matthew 6:33-34

> "But seek first the kingdom of God and His righteousness, and all these things shall be added to you. Therefore do not worry about tomorrow, for tomorrow will worry about its own things. Sufficient for the day is its own trouble."

In today's scripture, Jesus gives you not only a great reason **why** not to worry, but tells you **how** not to worry. Let's look at why you have no need to worry first.

It's unfortunate that when many become Christians, they are led to believe that they won't have any more problems. Nothing could be further from the truth! Each day has its own challenges. But the difference is that you now have God's wisdom and resources to overcome them. You have confidence that no matter what comes up in your day, you can handle it.

You've probably heard the saying, "Take one day at a time." That is the same guidance Jesus gives in the scriptures. It is futile to live in the past because it is gone and there is nothing you can do to change it. It is foolish to try to live in the future because it hasn't arrived yet, plus it is not promised to you. God has already determined the length of your days. You don't know when the end of them will be.

All you really have is today. So use your energy to enjoy it and make the most of it! One of the reasons I like to think of today as "the present" is that it helps me to remember that it is a gift. It is up to me to "unwrap" it by maximizing my time, keeping my attitude faith focused, and by seeking God's priorities, which is expanding His kingdom on Earth.

That leads to Jesus' direction on **how** to stop worrying – by occupying your mind and actions with seeking God's kingdom. What is God's kingdom? Romans 14:17 defines it: "for the kingdom of God is not eating and drinking, but righteousness and peace and joy in the Holy Spirit."

As a believer in Jesus Christ, you have the Holy Spirit living inside of you and dwelling with you (see John 14:16-18). So you can never say that you are alone when facing problems! Your willingness for the Holy Spirit to lead you is the key to living in righteousness, peace, and joy every day. As you learn how to listen to His voice and obey it, you will have new confidence that you are living out God's plan for your life.

When making your daily decisions, ask yourself, "Is this the right thing to do in God's sight?" Another good question to ask is, "Will this decision ultimately bring peace and joy?" Notice the word **ultimately**, which is important – especially when it comes to discipline.

Hebrews 12:11 is right when it says, "Now no chastening seems to be joyful for the present, but painful; nevertheless, afterward it yields the peaceable fruit of righteousness to those who have been trained by it."

Chastening is simply another word for "discipline." The Amplified Bible further clarifies what this scripture means regarding the peaceable fruit of righteousness: "...in conformity to God's will in purpose, thought, and action, resulting in right living and right standing with God."

Before I became a Christian, I used to think that the Christian life was boring. But now, I realize that each day is an adventure! You never know what person God will ask you to call, or speak to, or what new thing He may want to accomplish through you. When you occupy your mind with seeking God's kingdom daily, then you have no room in your life for worry!

Day 10: "But God..."

Today's focus scripture is taken from Psalm 43:5

"Why are you cast down, O my soul? And why are you disquieted within me? Hope in God; For I shall yet praise Him, The help of my countenance and my God."

[handwritten annotations: "over whelm in my self", "upset / worried inside myself", "feelings / pa"]

Isn't it comforting to know that even faithful men and women have periods of anxiety sometimes? King David was called "a man after God's own heart" not because God approved everything he did, but because David had a heart for pursuing God's presence and purpose for his life. He was quick to repent (turn around) when he messed up.

In this scripture, you see that David may have been down for the moment, but he didn't stay down! He reminded himself to hope in God and to praise. In doing so, he discovered that reflecting on the Lord's goodness lifted up his countenance – the expression on His face.

Author and bible teacher Joyce Meyer once said, "Some people who are saved need to notify their faces." They walk around as if they have no hope nor reason to praise. They might as well, at least in this circumstance, not even have God in their lives. All because they do not yet understand the concept of "**But God**."

What do I mean? "But God" means that your circumstances do not define you. They do not control your countenance nor your attitude. You recognize that God is the difference in every situation! He is the Alpha and Omega, the beginning and the end.

That's the part you may forget when you are anxious...to remember that God will see you through to the end.

You can say, "I'm not sure how I am going to pay my bills...**but God** will supply all of my needs according to His riches in glory by Christ Jesus."

You can say, "I am unmarried and feel so alone...**but God** has promised to never leave me nor forsake me."

You can say, "The doctor's report is not good...**but God** has promised to bring me health and healing and reveal to me the abundance of peace and truth."

Having a "But God" attitude is not about ignoring reality, but recognizing that circumstances are only **part** of reality! God's presence and wisdom are just as real and freely available for the believer in Jesus Christ!

You do yourself a great disservice by only living part of the story.

Instead, give yourself hope and lift up your countenance. Remind yourself of the **whole story**: With God in your life, your help is here and closer than a brother!

Day 11: Be Teachable

Today's focus scripture is taken from Psalm 90:12:

"So teach us to number our days,
That we may gain a heart of wisdom."

The bible says that our enemy, Satan, is the most cunning of all creatures.

I looked up *cunning* and it means "Having or showing skill in achieving one's ends by deceit or evasion." I think the one of biggest deceits the enemy commits is getting us to **devalue time**.

On the one hand, he says you don't have enough time to do things that matter to you. On the other hand, he makes you complacent by thinking you have all of the time in the world. As a result you procrastinate, i.e. "I'll do it tomorrow."

The Psalmist asks the Lord to teach him to number his days so that he gains a heart of wisdom. You can have the best teacher in the world (which you have in the Holy Spirit), but even the best teacher can't do much with a student who refuses to learn. How teachable are you? Do you learn from the mistakes of the past or do you make the same ones over and over?

I think your desire to learn and gain wisdom increases once you recognize that time is a finite resource. It is presumptuous to think that you have all the time in the world. The apostle James said it best, "Come now, you who say, 'Today or tomorrow we will go to such and such a city, spend a year there, buy and sell, and make a profit'; whereas you do not know what will happen tomorrow. For what is your life? It is even a vapor that appears for a little time and then vanishes away."

It's sobering to think of your life as a vapor. But consider the billions of people who have passed through life in the centuries before you. Only a few left behind a legacy from which

others benefited The rest were preoccupied with their own insecurities or the cares of this world. Instead of leaving behind footprints in the sand, they left butt prints in the sand – as author John Maxwell said so plainly!

You can relieve anxiety and gain confidence as you make an effort to use your time wisely each day. Invest each moment. Invest in renewing your mind and growing in the fruit of the Spirit (see Galatians 5:22-23). Most of all, invest in making others' lives better – even in small ways. *Love, joy, peace, patience, faithfulness, gentleness, self control, kindness*

The first step is to recognize the truth about time:

1. Enough time exists to do the things that God is calling you to do each day. Make those things priority. Taking care of your health is a wise priority because it empowers you to act with excellence.

2. Because your time is limited, refuse to waste it on unprofitable things. Many people

deal with anxiety because they spend major time on minor things.

Each day, commit to growing wiser so that you can leave a positive legacy to your loved ones and those God has placed in your life to influence!

Day 12: Make your Paths Straight

Today's focus scripture is taken from Proverbs 4:26

> "Ponder the path of your feet,
> And let all your ways be established."

A Chinese proverbs says, "The journey of a thousand miles begins with one step." But have you considered where your daily actions are taking you? As a believer in Jesus Christ and one who obeys His word, you know that your ultimate destination is heaven once this life is over. However to make your journey smoother, ask the Lord to help you follow a disciplined path today.

I once heard a pastor talking about the need for self-discipline to get delivered from things keeping you in bondage. When he said the word "discipline" I immediately thought about the word "disciple." What is a disciple? It is one who is being taught, a student.

With discipline must come a path of instruction!

Could your missing key to discipline be that you are so focused on what you don't want that you aren't following a daily path toward what you DO want?

You see, what you pay attention to increases in your experience. For example, if you tell yourself that you don't like being overweight, but do not provide a simple, easy path for yourself to eat healthier or exercise daily, then you won't change anything. As a result, what you don't want increases in your life.

You are both the student and the teacher when it comes to discipline. As a student, you might stumble along the path. That is where you as the teacher must step up. A good teacher is patient and helps the student either remove the obstacles that are in the way, go around the obstacles if they can't be removed, or take a different path altogether.

If you lack self-discipline, then all it means is that you have not given yourself a daily path of instruction to follow. The best path to create is one that is comprised of tiny steps:

- Want to eat healthier? Then your first tiny step could be getting rid of one soda in your home.

- Want to exercise? Then perhaps you can start by walking a short distance down the street when you get the mail everyday.

- Want to watch less television? Then just start with keeping the T.V. off for 10 minutes and work your way up

So today, think about your daily habits and identify which habit causes you the most anxiety. Target that habit to change. Create a new path of tiny steps that lead away from that habit and toward one that serves you better. Remove obstacles and temptations that may cause you to stumble and make your path straight. You will arrive at your new destination sooner than you think!

Day 13: The Lord is My Shepherd

Today's focus scripture is taken from Psalm 23:1

> "The Lord is my shepherd;
> I shall not want."

To remind myself that God is always with me, I often read Psalm 23. In the reprinting that follows, the words in italics are mine. They were impressed upon me during my prayer time many years ago.

Take time today to meditate on this word and let God's spirit refresh and restore you.

The LORD is my shepherd; – *The Lord takes care of me.*

I shall not want. – *He supplies all my needs according to His riches and glory.*

He makes me to lie down in green pastures; – *He grants me abundant prosperity.*

He leads me beside the still waters. *– He gives me peace that surpasses all understanding.*

He restores my soul; *– He calms and refreshes me.*

He leads me in the paths of righteousness *– He teaches me to live right according to His word.*

For His name's sake. *I represent Him in the world.*

Yea, though I walk through the valley of the shadow of death, *– Though I go through trials*

I will fear no evil; *– I will not allow fear, worry, doubt, depression, and discouragement to rule my mind.*

For You are with me; *– For God has promised to never to leave me nor forsake me.*

Your rod and Your staff, they comfort me. *– He protects and strengthens me.*

You prepare a table before me in the presence of my enemies; *– His goodness towards me shall be clearly seen.*

You anoint my head with oil; *– I shall rejoice in His continual presence.*

My cup runs over. – *He has opened his good treasure for me.*

Surely goodness and mercy shall follow me – *Goodness and mercy follows me all the days of my life because the Lord is good and merciful.*

All the days of my life;

And I will dwell in the house of the LORD – *And I have everlasting life because of the finished work of my Savior.*

Forever.

Day 14: "Nothing is Too Hard..."

Today's focus scripture is taken from Genesis 18:14

18: 1-14

"Is anything too hard for the Lord?"

In my opinion, this is the greatest question ever asked! It is fitting that the Lord asked it of Abraham, the father of faith. God told Abraham that his wife Sarah would have a son. Now Sarah was old and barren, well past the age when she would have been capable of bearing children. When Sarah, who was in the tent eavesdropping on their conversation, heard the Lord say that she would have a son, she laughed.

I'm sure most of us can identify with her response simply because in the natural, having a baby many years past menopause is impossible. But with God...you probably know how I'm going to finish that sentence!

Sarah was 90 years old when her son, Issac, was born. Abraham was 100 years old. The Lord's word came to pass exactly as He said it would.

I think the main reason we miss out on having God's best in our lives is that we get impatient during the wait. We think it is taking too long for God's word to come to pass and feel our hope fading.

If you find yourself thinking about the size of the problem and feeling hopeless, let that be your cue for a reality check. You are probably comparing yourself with the problem – and seeing how inadequate your resources are to deal with it.

But change the script and start comparing God with the problem. However big it is, your God is bigger! Re-affirm His stature in your mind. Remind yourself of all the great things God has done for you in the past. Remind yourself of His mighty deeds in the Bible: He parted the Red Sea, helped His people defeat countless enemies, restored sight to blinded eyes, made the lame walk, and raised people from the dead.

Whatever seemingly impossible situation you are facing, it is no match for Him.

Ask yourself, "Is anything too hard for the Lord?" When you know God, you can shout with confidence, "No!"

Day 15: Make your Heart Merry

Happy

Today's focus scripture is taken from Proverbs 17:22

"A merry heart does good, like medicine,
But a broken spirit dries the bones."

If you are dealing with anxiety, you may think, "What reason do I have to be joyful?" I want you to meditate on the following scripture for a moment: "Therefore, if anyone is in Christ, he is a new creation; old things have passed away; behold, all things have become new (2 Corinthians 5:17)."

Since you have accepted Jesus as your Savior, this applies to you! Your sins have been washed away and your heart overflows with rivers of living water through the indwelling of the Holy Spirit (see John 7:38).

This wonderful fact makes me think about the lyrics to the song "O Happy Day:"

Oh happy day (oh happy day)
Oh happy day (oh happy day)
When Jesus washed (when Jesus washed)
When Jesus washed (when Jesus washed)
Jesus washed (when Jesus washed)
Washed my sins away (oh happy day)
Oh happy day (oh happy day)

Ask the Holy Spirit in prayer right now to fill your heart to overflowing with His presence. Ask Him to fill you with the joy of your Salvation and your new life in Christ. No longer will you feel broken and dry routinely. You have the Great Physician ready to heal every ache and pain associated with a broken spirit (mind, will, and emotions).

He has made a river in your barren situation. Can't you feel it flowing?

Meditate on Jesus' goodness and you will make your heart merry!

Day 16: Acceptable Meditation

Today's focus scripture is taken from Psalm 19:14

"Let the words of my mouth and the meditation of my heart Be acceptable in Your sight, O Lord, my strength and my Redeemer."

Why is the meditation of your heart so important? Jesus taught in Matthew 15:18-20: "...For out of the heart proceed evil thoughts, murders, adulteries, fornications, thefts, false witness, blasphemies. These are the things which defile a man..."

You can't help fleeting thoughts, but you can choose whether to permit them to live with you! When thoughts contrary to God's word visit your mind like an unwanted house guest, what do you do?

- Do you remind them of truth from God's word and evict them?

- Or do you permit them to move in, allowing them to influence your emotions, intellect, and morals?

When the bible refers to the *heart* of man, it means more than just your feelings; It means the center of your inner life: your emotions, intellect, and morals together.

Think of it this way: A house has two main parts, the outside (which is what people see) and the inside. It is the inside that is most important. Why? Because it is where you spend most of your time. Proper management of it helps ensure that everything else operates efficiently. What good does it do to have a good-looking outside, but the inside is a hot mess? When the inside of a home is peaceful and well-ordered, it improves the quality of your whole life.

What is acceptable Christian meditation according to the Lord? Philippians 4:8 gives you guidance: "Finally, brethren, whatever things are true, whatever things are noble, whatever things are just, whatever things are pure, whatever things are lovely, whatever things are of good report, if there is any virtue and if there is anything praiseworthy—meditate on these things."

Everything related to Jesus fits this description. This is a meditation God gave me:

- **True:** Jesus is the living Word and His word is true.
- **Noble:** Jesus sacrificed Himself on the cross for my sins.
- **Just:** Jesus paid for my sin debt, so I am no longer condemned under the law.
- **Pure:** Jesus lived a sinless life and He is my ultimate role model on how to live right.
- **Lovely:** I love Jesus because He first loved me.
- **Good report:** Hallelujah, I have overcome the world through Jesus!

- **Virtue:** I am being transformed into Jesus' virtuous image from glory to glory.
- **Praiseworthy:** I am seated in heavenly places in Christ and He lives in me now and forever.

Meditating on Jesus is the surefire way to ensure your meditation is acceptable in God's sight. When you do this, the peace of God will guard your heart and mind – through Christ Jesus!

Day 17: Practice Contentment

Today's focus scripture is taken
from Philippians 4:11-12

"...for I have learned in whatever state I
am, to be content: I know how to be
abased, and I know how to abound.
Everywhere and in all things I have
learned both to be full and to be hungry,
both to abound and to suffer need."

If anybody knows how to go through trying
times, it's the apostle Paul – the writer of the
book of Philippians. Some of the things he
went through are described in 2 Corinthians
11:24-28:

"From the Jews five times I received
forty stripes minus one. Three times I
was beaten with rods; once I was
stoned; three times I was shipwrecked; a
night and a day I have been in the deep;

in journeys often, in perils of waters, in perils of robbers, in perils of my own countrymen, in perils of the Gentiles, in perils in the city, in perils in the wilderness, in perils in the sea, in perils among false brethren; in weariness and toil, in sleeplessness often, in hunger and thirst, in fastings often, in cold and nakedness—besides the other things, what comes upon me daily: my deep concern for all the churches."

And yet for all his suffering, this was the same man who also wrote about being content! Was he crazy? A glutton for punishment? No! The reason Paul was able to maintain his peace is found in the last sentence: "...my deep concern for all the churches."

You see, the secret of being content is in the same word: *content.* In this context, it is pronounced differently – as CON-tent. Here, I'm using it to mean "contained within; part of a larger whole." Paul was able to stay peaceful because he saw meaning in the trials he went through. He saw himself as contained within the family of God, part of God's plan to equip the churches and spread the gospel.

To practice contentment, follow Paul's example. What you are going through is temporary, a light affiliation. As part of the family of God, He has a purpose and a plan for you. You can be content when you focus on the big picture – His glory, not your comfort.

As you allow the Holy Spirit to work in you, you will start to see more of the fruit of His Spirit manifested in your life: You'll have more love, joy, peace, patience, kindness, goodness, faithfulness, gentleness, and self control.

By this, God is glorified. There is no greater source of contentment than to know that you are becoming everything the Creator had in mind when He created you!

.

Day 18: Call Him Up!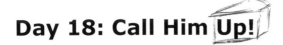

Today's focus scripture is taken
from Deuteronomy 4:7

> "For what great nation is there that has
> God so near to it, as the Lord our God is
> to us, for whatever reason we may call
> upon Him?"

I love that our God has an open door policy!
Today's scripture reminds you of two facts:
God is near you and you may call him for any
reason. Did you get that last part? You can
call up the One who created the Universe – the
mountains, the stars, the oceans, and you. His
generosity is too wonderful for me to fully
comprehend, even now. But you better believe
I take full advantage of the open door!

I used to delay my calls to the Lord. I'd
worship Him just on Sunday and then put Him
on the shelf Monday through Saturday. I
thought that I needed to try to handle things

on my own and only call on the Lord as my last resort.

But once I learned that God says that we may call upon Him for any reason, then I decided to put it to the test. I started involving the Lord in my daily life. I asked Him for His wisdom in the daily challenges I faced. I asked him "What should I do in this situation?" or "What should I say to this person?" In my communications with Him, my purpose is to get guidance on how to bring Him glory not to complain.

The difference in the Christian faith is that we Believers have a relationship, not a just a religion. Think about your most intimate relationships. How strong would they be if your only communication with that person was few and far between?

The emotional distance would soon cause you to drift apart.

Don't allow yourself to drift away from the Lord. He longs to hear from you. Even though

He already knows everything that is going on with you, it pleases Him when one of His children takes a step of trust to confide in Him.

Have you called on the Lord today? He's waiting to hear from you!

Day 19: Start your Morning Blessed

Today's focus scripture is taken from Psalm 5:3

"My voice You shall hear in the morning, O Lord; In the morning I will direct it to You, And I will look up."

Imagine this: You go to the airport and step up to the airline ticket counter. The service representative asks, "Where are you going today?"

You reply, "I don't know."

The airline representative looks at you as if you've lost your mind.

Do you drift through each day with no idea of where you are going? Or do you know where you want to go, but have not taken time to develop daily habits that will get you there?

The scenario I described is the same as approaching each day without goals. However, if you have a goal but are not practicing habits that lead to that goal, it's like getting a ticket, but not bothering to get on the plane!

One of the best goals you can have is to strengthen your relationship with God. And one of the best habits you can develop to reach that goal is to spend time with God first thing in the morning!

You will be amazed at the difference this makes, especially if you are accustomed to starting your morning with negative self talk like, "I don't feel like going to work today" or worse, watching the morning news. The latter is especially damaging because the news is typically 95% bad news – full of stories of man's inhumanity to man. You start your day in a depressed position.

But expressing your gratitude to God and receiving strength from Him puts you in a blessed position. In God's presence is full of joy and that joy will enable you to face the world with your head held high, secure in His love.

Another good thing to do to start your morning blessed is to take time to decide on the things that you value in life and then write down 5 things you want to accomplish that are consistent with those values. If you have difficulty with this, then ask the Lord in prayer to direct your steps according to His word.

Instead of drifting aimlessly, your days will become more meaningful. You'll also be excited when you experience yourself getting closer to your destination with each passing day.

Day 20: Discipline your Body

Today's focus scripture is taken from 1 Corinthians 9:27

"But I discipline my body and bring it into subjection, lest, when I have preached to others, I myself should become disqualified."

The Greek ideal of health is a sound mind in a sound body. While we've spent most of our time discussing the importance of renewing your mind to God's word, taking care of your body is important too. After all, it's the only vehicle you have to occupy while you are on this Earth.

Wherever your mind wants to go, your body has to take you there. If your body can't move, your mind is not going anywhere physically, no matter how much it might want to go!

The hierarchy of decision making for a Christian should be this:

- Spirit — *how* God is leading us
- Soul (mind, will, emotions)
- Body — *Physical wellbeing*

That is, the Spirit should control what you do in your body and mind. However what often happens is we live our lives like this:

- Soul — *emotions*
- Body — *impact -*
- Spirit — *God*

In other words, we allow our feelings to control what we do with our bodies – the same as the World does. Our Spirit man often has little say in it.

The reason this is a mistake is that your feelings often come from old thoughts and memories. You are often driven to recreate old pleasurable experiences – even if those experiences weren't ultimately good for you. Back in the 60's, there was a popular philosophy: "If it feels good, do it."

Well, excessive eating feels good. So does excessive drinking or drugs – or so I've read. However all of these behaviors will ultimate destroy your body's ability to respond to Spiritual demands. It will impact your ability to fulfill your God given purpose.

Your body will be too busy using its energy to REPAIR the excesses of your indulgence – it won't have the energy to do much else!

That's why Paul in this scripture says that he disciplines his body. The translation of this scripture in the New Living Translation says, "I discipline my body like an athlete, training it to do what it should. Otherwise, I fear that after preaching to others I myself might be disqualified."

I'm sure sometime in your life you have watched the Olympics. Do you think Olympians spend that season binge drinking, overeating, or doing illegal drugs? No, because they know that those activities have a physical cost – one that they cannot afford since their goal is to win.

Jesus' commissioned His disciples in Matthew 28:19-20 to go and make disciples of all the nations and to teach them how to live according to the way Jesus taught. Are you fulfilling this commission? Now you may not have been called to go to a foreign country on a missionary trip, but you've certainly been called to minister to those within your circle of influence: family, friends, coworkers, employees, acquaintances.

The poorer your health becomes, the more limited your reach. The motivational speaker Jim Rohn once said, "Some people don't do well because they don't feel well." Do everything possible to renew your mind to God's word so that you can discipline your body accordingly. God's overall will concerning your body's health is this:

"Beloved, I pray that you may prosper in all things and be in health, just as your soul prospers (3 John 1:2)." This means that God wants you healthy in Spirit, soul, and body. So by making positive health choices, you are fulfilling God's will in this matter.

As I mentioned, most people fulfill **their own will** in how they manage their bodies – seeking what is pleasurable in the short-term regardless of the long-term consequences. What can make the process of changing your health choices easier is to build pleasure into your daily life rather than seeking thrills in excess.

Make a list of those things you find pleasurable. Some of those things can be:

- Funny movies
- Laughter
- Good music
- Using a foot roller
- Warm baths with candles
- Stretching out your body

- Dancing
- Learning something interesting and new

All of these things stimulate the brain's pleasure center. It is the same mechanism that drives people to eat or drink too much, or do drugs. However, the above things will **give** you energy rather than drain it.

So if you currently have habits of excess in your life, then you can start to reverse it by making sure you give yourself healthier ways to feel good in your daily life.

Not only does this make life more enjoyable, but your new disciplined body will be able to respond instantly to the Father's call, whatever it may be!

Day 21: Avoid Temptation

Today's focus scripture is taken from Luke 22:40

> "...Pray that you may not enter into temptation."

Besides today's focus scripture, Jesus advised believers to pray to avoid temptation at least 2 other times in the scriptures:

- "...And do not lead us into temptation, But deliver us from the evil one (Luke 11:4)"
- "...Rise and pray, lest you enter into temptation (Luke 22:46)"

Every morning in my prayer time with my husband, I always pray that we not be led into temptation and delivered from evil. The truth is that I don't have time to deal with the enemy messing with me for his own amusement. I'm busy working to living a life that pleases God.

I've discovered my God-given purpose and want to get on with fulfilling it unhindered.

I have no time for the enemy's lies either. I spent too many years believing them, stealing valuable time that could have been spent growing in the knowledge of God, and growing in Spiritual fruit (love, joy, peace, etc).

You don't have time for that either. You've got places to go and people to see!

Now, I don't mind if the trial I am going through is one that God has allowed because it will ultimately bring him glory. But I am a big believer in a principle I learned from the martial arts: "The best way to win a fight is to avoid getting into one in the first place." If there is a way to avoid temptation or being the target of the devil's evil schemes, then I want that protection.

Because God knows everything that is going to happen to me each day, I always ask him to lead me away from temptation and deliver me from the plans of the evil one.

Think about your typical day. Are there poor health habits to which you are in bondage? Do you have problems controlling your anger? Are you frequently depressed?

If you have these or other areas that cause you anxiety, then start asking God to help you avoid those temptations. In this way, you can stop anxiety-producing situations before they even start!

Day 22: Hope in your Future

Today's focus scripture is taken from Jeremiah 29:11

> "For I know the thoughts that I think toward you, says the Lord, thoughts of peace and not of evil, to give you a future and a hope."

Doesn't it feel good to know that God thinks about you and that He already has a future planned for you? It gives me great peace to know that I may not know every detail of what He has in store for me, but I know it is going to be good! How can I have that confidence?

Because I know that I serve a good God. No, better than good. He's great, awesome, marvelous, mighty, righteous...there aren't enough superlatives to describe Him. On second thought, there is one:

Holy.

Because God is Holy, he cannot be judged by human standards. He is perfect and cannot lie, so when He says He has a hope and future for you, then you can count on it.

If you are connected to the Lord through daily, personal relationship then you can be confident that He will give you the desires of your heart. By that, I mean that your desires will be consistent with His perfect will and perfect word.

Check out the desires of your heart right now. Are they consistent with God's word?

For example, if you desire a husband but you are engaged to an unsaved man, then that future is not of God (see 2 Corinthians 6:14 and Amos 3:3).

On the other hand, if you desire a business, serving your community using your God-given talents then that is consistent with a God-given future. All you need to do is ask the Lord in prayer for the resources to start and wisdom on timing.

One of the Holy Spirit's roles in your life is to tell you things to come (see John 16:13). ← guide you to him While the Lord may not give you His entire plan, He will certainly direct you to the next step. When you take that step in faith, then He will reveal the next step to you, directing your path (see Matthew 25:14-29). Take what is given to you and grow,

If you are currently worried about the future, then pray to the Lord about this concern, asking Him to give you His peace. Re-affirm His promise of hope and a future in your mind. You likely will need to do this often to renew your mind from those old worrying patterns.

Remind yourself that because you know God's character, He does not make promises that He doesn't keep. He is faithful!

Day 23: Peace Like a River

Today's focus scripture is taken from Isaiah
48:18

> *followed*
> "Oh, that you had heeded My
> commandments! Then your peace would
> have been like a river, And your
> righteousness like the waves of the sea."

Can you hear the pleading in this scripture?
The prophet Isaiah was delivering a message
to the people of Israel, who had turned away
from God and toward false gods. Judgment
upon the nation was imminent; the Lord had
warned the people that if they continued to be
disobedient, He would remove the hedge of
protection around them and other nations
would overtake them. But the people did not
listen and disaster came upon them.

Isaiah says in the scripture that if the people
had heeded the Lord's commandments, they
would have experienced peace like a river.
Have you ever gone on a walk by a river or a
lake? Just being in the presence of the gentle

waves brings peace. Whenever you are feeling anxious or stressed, it is a good idea to get into nature and experience the natural beauty of God's creation. It will help you regain perspective about what is really important in life.

In contrast, Isaiah says that in obeying God's commandments, the righteousness of His people would be like the waves of the sea. While rivers and seas are both bodies of water, a sea has more power behind it.

In order for you to operate in righteousness, you need power to overcome the snares of the enemy. When you obey the Holy Spirit's leading, you have His power available to you, which is just as awesome and relentless as the waves of the sea.

This is an incredible combination: You have peace inwardly and power outwardly to deal with your circumstances. Both of these are contingent upon obedience. If you lack peace and power in your daily life, then meditate on this scripture. Do you have any areas of disobedience in your life? Ask the Lord to search your heart and lead you in His way so that you can prosper in every area!

Day 24: Bold in your Soul

Today's focus scripture is taken from Psalm
138:3

> "In the day when I cried out, You
> answered me,
> *And* made me bold *with* strength in
> my soul.

My pastor included this scripture in our bible
study recently and at the end of his teaching,
he had us shout, "Lord, make me bold with
strength in my soul!" I challenge you to do the
same thing. It feels good!

If you are overwhelmed with anxiety, what is
preventing you from crying out to the Lord?
You might think that He would get tired of
hearing from you, but nowhere in the bible do
I see God refusing to answer someone whose
heart was genuinely seeking Him.

The only other reason I can think of that would
keep someone from crying out to the Lord is

99

pride. The person may think that they don't need Him and are capable of handling the situation for themselves. But life has a way of bringing to your knees. When you've reached the end of yourself, then God is there to give you a new beginning.

Where once there was fear, He provides courage; you once were anxious, but now there is peace; you once were timid, but now you are bold – able to meet the challenges of life because you know that God is holding you up and holding you together.

You need Him to strengthen you in your soul because negative influences can take their toll on your mind, will, and emotions. When your soul is unstable, it can cause you to make rash decisions or have devastating knee-jerk reactions to others. However, when God strengthens you in your soul, you can respond to circumstances with grace and have the boldness to testify to others of all that the Lord has done for you!

Day 25: Strength in the WORD

Today's focus scripture is taken from Psalm 119:28

Sorryo

"My soul melts from heaviness;

Strengthen me according to Your word."

Psalm 119 is the longest chapter in the bible and I don't believe that is an accident; after all, the chapter is all about the benefits of God's word. It is essential for living a victorious Christian life. In today's scripture, the Psalmist prays to the Lord to strengthen Him according to His word. What are some other benefits of the WORD – as stated in this Psalm?

- Cleanses your way
- Revives you
- Enables you to receive salvation
- Reminds you of God's mercy
- Teaches you good judgment and knowledge
- Comforts you

- Upholds you
- Reminds you of God's lovingkindness
- Gives you understanding
- Delivers you

If you do not have a time of regular bible study in your day, then you are leaving all of these benefits on the table! You've probably noticed that many of the scriptures I've referenced in this series come from the book of Psalm. If you are dealing with anxiety in this season, then I recommend using Psalm for regular study. These men knew what it takes to successfully go through!

The book of Psalm follows the book of Job. It occurred to me years ago that God in His wisdom ordered the book of ultimate comfort to follow the book of ultimate suffering. While none of us will ever experience suffering on the magnitude that Job did, many of us have experienced the heartbreak of losing loved ones, financial challenges, or physical infirmities at various times in our lives. It's part of this fallen world in which we live.

Someday, if you are in Christ, you can look forward to joining with the Lord for all eternity. All of these trials will become a distant memory. God has promised to wipe away your tears. Until then, you have the comfort of the Lord's presence through prayer and can receive strength through His word. Receive it.

Day 26: You're Enlisted

Today's focus scripture is taken from 2
Timothy 2:3-4

> "You therefore must endure hardship as
> a good soldier of Jesus Christ. No one
> engaged in warfare entangles himself
> with the affairs of this life, that he may
> please him who enlisted him as a
> soldier."

"Trouble doesn't come to last, but to pass." I
heard that saying from some of the older
ladies in my church growing up and didn't
know what it meant then, but I do now.

I've come to say, "This too shall pass"
whenever hardship comes my way. Sometimes
when you are dealing with challenging
situations, the enemy can trick you into
believing that just because you are
experiencing trouble now means that it will
always be so. But that is a lie. Within the

biblical directive to **endure** hardship is the word **end**. When you take time to remind yourself that the hard situation is destined to end, it makes it easier to endure!

The other secret of enduring is found in today's scripture also: Your ultimate mission is to please God in the way you live. After all, at the end of this life, you will be judged on how well you used the resources God gave you. So like a soldier you must stay focused on your ultimate mission and not allow anything to deter you from that.

Matthew 13:22 warns of this danger: "Now he who received seed among the thorns is he who hears the word, and the cares of this world and the deceitfulness of riches choke the word, and he becomes unfruitful."

To deal with the cares of this world – cast the burden onto the Lord.

To avoid the deceitfulness of riches, remind yourself that money is not your source. God is your source and Him only shall you worship.

You've been enlisted to bear fruit that will glorify God in your body and Spirit. Stay focused on this mission and you will never fail!

Day 27: Joyful Discipline

Today's focus scripture is taken from Hebrews 12:11

punsiment

> "Now no chastening seems to be joyful for the present, but painful; nevertheless, afterward it yields the peaceable fruit of righteousness to those who have been trained by it."

You probably read the title of today's devotion and did a double take. How can discipline be joyful? After all, doesn't discipline mean that you trying to make yourself do what you don't want to do?

That what most people think about discipline...which is why they avoid it. But I challenge you to see things differently. I want you to look beyond the obvious.

In the scripture, the term *chastening* is a synonym for discipline. Examine the scripture closely; it says that discipline doesn't seem to be joyful in the present but painful. The key phrase is **seems to be.** That means in the moment when you are exerting self-discipline in a particular area, the pain is not reality; joy is reality!

The pain is really just a temporary sting. However, the results that come from enduring the sting are permanent.

Whenever you are working to change established habits, there is always tension between the person you are and the person you want to be. That tension is manifested in your body and it feels uncomfortable. Think about a little child about to get a vaccination. When they see the needle, all sorts of horrors go through their mind about the pain to come. They react based on that **imagined horror** rather than reality itself.

In reality, the needle only enters their body for seconds. It may sting for a few moments, but afterwards they will be protected from life-threatening diseases for years to come or even a lifetime. Joy!

Consider this:

- As a disciple of Christ, God is conforming you into His image. Your old, fleshly self doesn't like it one bit.
- You are working to change your health for the better. Your flesh doesn't like that either.
- You are taking steps to control your spending. Ouch! Your flesh says "Stop it – spend, spend, spend!"

Now suppose you did what your flesh wanted in these situations. What would be the likely result?

- Carnal Christian
- Sick, infirm, or in bondage to bad habits
- In debt

When you look at it this way, doesn't it make you wonder whose side the flesh is on?

You know whose side it is on! So why do you keep making the enemy's job easier through your cooperation? Stick him!

Learn to enjoy those little stings because they are Spiritual in nature. We are told that the sword of the Spirit is the word of God. Every time you obey the word (use the sword), it is a strike against the enemy.

Look past the sting and see the victory beyond. Discipline is worth celebrating!

Day 28: "I'm Blessed!"

Today's focus scripture is taken from 2 Peter 1:2-4

> "Grace and peace be multiplied to you in the knowledge of God and of Jesus our Lord, as His divine power has given to us all things that pertain to life and godliness, through the knowledge of Him who called us by glory and virtue, by which have been given to us exceedingly great and precious promises, that through these you may be partakers of the divine nature, having escaped the corruption that is in the world through lust."

I teach Sunday School for adult women at my local church and one of the lessons I taught recently was on 2 Peter 1:4-14. The apostle Peter wrote these scriptures as his last will and testament.

The Romans were persecuting Christians and Peter knew that he was a prime target; God had shown him that he was going to die soon. So Peter was determined to use the time he had left to remind his fellow Believers (which includes you) about what it takes to live a life that pleases God – to live in God's blessings.

I believe most Christians want this goal. In the focus scripture, Peter says that God has given you precious promises by which you may be partakers of the divine nature. This means that you have the opportunity to participate in God's plan through faith when you believe in His promises.

You can return to Eden (in a manner of speaking), walking with God daily and coming to know Him, just as the first man Adam did in the beginning.

In the commentary on the lesson I taught, I read this wonderful statement: "Just as natural as it is for us to breathe, it is as natural for God to bless." Hallelujah!

Take a deep inhale right now. On the exhale, say out loud, "I'm blessed."

In the scripture, Peter expresses His desire that grace and peace be multiplied to you in the knowledge of Jesus. One of the Holy Spirit's roles is to create the character of Christ within you. As you listen to His voice and obey it, grace and peace will be multiplied to you.

Take a deep inhale right now. On the exhale, say out loud, "I'm blessed."

Scripture also says that you have been called to glorify God by Jesus' glory and virtue. How beautiful is our Savior. How magnificent, awesome, powerful! To think that you were created for such a time as this, to display His glory to a dark and hurting world. I hope this fact puts you in awe as much as it does me.

Take a deep inhale right now. On the exhale, say out loud, "I'm blessed."

I hope after reflecting on these facts that you will agree with the old adage: "Too blessed to be stressed." You are also "too blessed to be anxious" and "too blessed to be fearful."

God has given you everything you need to grow in the knowledge of Him and to live in godliness. Now, walk in your blessings!

Day 29: Fullness of Joy

Today's focus scripture is taken from Psalm 16:11

> "You will show me the path of life; In Your presence is fullness of joy; At Your right hand are pleasures forevermore."

Who wants to live a more abundant life? Living in bondage to anxiety, fear, worry, and depression is not what God wants for you. Instead in this scripture, you are promised that God will show you the path of life.

John 17:3 defines what it means to have life: "And this is eternal life, that they may know You, the only true God, and Jesus Christ whom You have sent."

You may be going through difficult circumstances right now, but your circumstances do not define your life. Make that clear in your mind. However, taking time to experience God's presence adds life to your life.

Do you have an appointed time every day to meet with the Lord quietly?

If you have lack in your life, it's time to fill yourself up! Enter God's presence with thanksgiving and praise first. Then, quiet your mind, inviting God to speak to you. This is not as easy as it sounds because the noise from modern distractions (television, computers, cell phone) can drown out your ability to hear the voice of the Lord. So you need to take steps to reconnect to your source of life deliberately.

Even 5-minutes of "re-fueling time" daily is better than nothing. However, the more quiet time you can build into your day, the better. As you listen to the Lord speak during this time, you give Him space to provide solutions to the problems you face and give you a higher perspective. You will come away from this time feeling more relaxed, confident, and joyful.

You may have come to the Lord feeling empty, but He will never let you leave His presence empty! He is a God of abundance so get ready to receive to your fullest capacity. You will increase your capacity as you humble yourself, submit to God's leading, and obey His direction.

Day 30: Remain Planted

Today's focus scripture is taken from Jeremiah 17:8

> "For he shall be like a tree planted by the waters, Which spreads out its roots by the river, And will not fear when heat comes; But its leaf will be green, And will not be anxious in the year of drought, Nor will cease from yielding fruit."

In this final scripture in the 'Anxiety Relief' series, you have a picture of a flourishing life in Christ. The images described reveal a life that is:

- Free from fear and anxiety
- Healthy
- Fruitful

But in order for this picture to come to pass, certain conditions must exist:

121

- **You must be planted.** Each day, take time to plant God's word in your heart. Meditate on the word to the point where you see a picture of it coming to pass in your life. If doubts come up, re-affirm your belief in the truth of that word. This is the equivalent of pulling up weeds or clearing away thorns in a garden.
- **You must stay connected to your source.** The Holy Spirit will make the word of God come alive to you. He will refresh you, revive you, and bring you peace. Practice the presence of God through daily prayer, praise, and worship.

Your change may not come immediately, but it will come. God promises that His word will not come back to Him void (see Isaiah 55:11). Jesus has given you the victory in every situation. So take one day at a time. Like seeds in the natural, you won't see the growth happening beneath the surface, but one day you see the manifestation of the seed's promise.

God has a great plan for your life. Be anxious for nothing; in everything, pray!

About the Author

"Just wanted to again thank you for sharing your unique and engaging presentation to help us take back our temples! You were truly a blessing and I know that many were enlightened by what you shared."

- Danese Turner, Turner Chapel AME, Marietta GA

Kimberly Taylor is the creator of **Takebackyourtemple.com**, a website that inspires Christians to Spiritual, emotional, and physical health. She is the author of the ebook *Take Back Your Temple* and the books ***The Weight Loss scriptures, God's Word is Food***, and **many others**.

Once 240 pounds and a size 22, Kim lost 85 pounds through renewing her mind and taking action upon God's word. Her experience led her to establish the Take Back Your Temple website. "Take Back Your Temple" is a prayer that asks God to take control of your body and your life so He can use them for His purpose and agenda.

Kim's weight loss success story has been featured on CBN's *The 700 Club,* and in *Prevention Magazine, Essence Magazine, Charisma Magazine* and many other magazines and newspapers. She has also been interviewed on various radio programs.

Kim exhorts people of faith to become good stewards of all the resources God has given to them, including time, money, talents, and physical health. "I am passionate about empowering others to adopt healthy lifestyles so they can fulfill their God-given purpose," she says.

"My dream is for God's people to stand apart because we are healthy, prosperous and living the abundant life to which we are called. I want non-believers to look at us and want what we have: Spiritual, mental, and physical wholeness. Then when they ask us what we are doing differently, we can tell them about Jesus, the author and finisher of our faith."

Stay Connected

You can stay connected with Kimberly Taylor through the following channels:

Amazon Author Page

You can learn about all of Kimberly Taylor's books and eBooks available on Amazon.com at one convenient location: **https://www.amazon.com/author/kimberlyytaylor**

Take Back Your Temple website

Kimberly's website, **www.takebackyourtemple.com/** shares her testimony of deliverance from emotional overeating through the change God made in her heart and mind. Hundreds of free articles on the website encourage other Christians on the road to Spiritual, emotional, and physical health.

Facebook

You can connect with Kimberly on Facebook at **http://www.facebook.com/takebackyourtemple**. She also moderates a secret Facebook support group comprised of believers who struggle with emotional eating and are working to change their health. Details on how to join the group are available at *takebackyourtemple.com*.

Twitter

Follow Kimberly on Twitter at **twitter.com/tbytkimberly**

Pinterest

You can view Kim's Pinterest boards at
http://pinterest.com/tbyt/

All paperback versions of the *Bible Study for Women* series were published through **StartYourBook.org**.